This Book Belongs To

_____

_____

_____

How To Use Plane Spotting Log Book

This plane spotting log book is a great way to record your planeWatching hobby. It is a ideal book if you are a plane spotter and want to Track aircraft for personal use or asa a professional.

Each page has 5 parts to record:

Aircraft Spotted

Record date, time, location and details of the airport.

Aircraft Information

All aircraft and engine information line aircraft name, model, type, weight, capacity, length, wing area, launched in, engine type, engine no, livery, height, wing shape, useiage Diameter, based on, first flight etc are record here.

Weather

Select the weather condition from given weather status.

Equipment Used

What type of equipment use in the plane

Notes

Write a short note or thoughts which are not of the aircraft that was spotted

This log book is a great way to keep all of your important information in one place. Also simple and easy to use.

✈ Aircraft Spotted ✈

Date/Time: _____ Where/Location: _____

Airport Details: _____

✈ Aircraft Information ✈

Aircraft Name: _____ Engine Type: _____

Aircraft Model: _____ Engine No: _____

Aircraft Type: _____ Livery: _____

Aircraft Weight: _____ Height: _____

Aircraft Capacity: _____ Wing Shape: _____

Aircraft Length: _____ Fuseiage Diameter: _____

Wing Area: _____ Based On: _____

Launched In: _____ First Flight: _____

✈ Weather ✈

Clean ☐   Sunny ☐   Stormy ☐   Rainy ☐   Cloudy ☐

✈ Equipment Used ✈

_____

_____

_____

✈ Notes ✈

_____

_____

_____

 Aircraft Spotted ✈

Date/Time: _____ Where/Location: _____

Airport Details: _____

✈ Aircraft Information ✈

Aircraft Name: _____ Engine Type: _____

Aircraft Model: _____ Engine No: _____

Aircraft Type: _____ Livery: _____

Aircraft Weight: _____ Height: _____

Aircraft Capacity: _____ Wing Shape: _____

Aircraft Length: _____ Fuseiage Diameter: _____

Wing Area: _____ Based On: _____

Launched In: _____ First Flight: _____

✈ Weather ✈

Clean ☐   Sunny ☐   Stormy ☐   Rainy ☐   Cloudy ☐

✈ Equipment Used ✈

_____

_____

_____

✈ Notes ✈

_____

_____

_____

✈ Aircraft Spotted ✈

Date/Time: _____ Where/Location: _____

Airport Details: _____

✈ Aircraft Information ✈

Aircraft Name: _____ Engine Type: _____

Aircraft Model: _____ Engine No: _____

Aircraft Type: _____ Livery: _____

Aircraft Weight: _____ Height: _____

Aircraft Capacity: _____ Wing Shape: _____

Aircraft Length: _____ Fuseiage Diameter: _____

Wing Area: _____ Based On: _____

Launched In: _____ First Flight: _____

✈ Weather ✈

Clean ☐   Sunny ☐   Stormy ☐   Rainy ☐   Cloudy ☐

✈ Equipment Used ✈

_____

_____

_____

✈ Notes ✈

_____

_____

_____

_____

✈ Aircraft Spotted ✈

Date/Time: _____   Where/Location: _____

Airport Details: _____

✈ Aircraft Information ✈

Aircraft Name: _____   Engine Type: _____

Aircraft Model: _____   Engine No: _____

Aircraft Type: _____   Livery: _____

Aircraft Weight: _____   Height: _____

Aircraft Capacity: _____   Wing Shape: _____

Aircraft Length: _____   Fuseiage Diameter: _____

Wing Area: _____   Based On: _____

Launched In: _____   First Flight: _____

✈ Weather ✈

Clean ☐   Sunny ☐   Stormy ☐   Rainy ☐   Cloudy ☐

✈ Equipment Used ✈

_____

_____

_____

✈ Notes ✈

_____

_____

_____

✈ Aircraft Spotted ✈

Date/Time: _____ Where/Location: _____

Airport Details: _____

✈ Aircraft Information ✈

Aircraft Name: _____ Engine Type: _____

Aircraft Model: _____ Engine No: _____

Aircraft Type: _____ Livery: _____

Aircraft Weight: _____ Height: _____

Aircraft Capacity: _____ Wing Shape: _____

Aircraft Length: _____ Fuseiage Diameter: _____

Wing Area: _____ Based On: _____

Launched In: _____ First Flight: _____

✈ Weather ✈

Clean ☐   Sunny ☐   Stormy ☐   Rainy ☐   Cloudy ☐

✈ Equipment Used ✈

✈ Notes ✈

✈ Aircraft Spotted ✈

Date/Time: .... Where/Location: ....

Airport Details: ....

✈ Aircraft Information ✈

Aircraft Name: .... Engine Type: ....

Aircraft Model: .... Engine No: ....

Aircraft Type: .... Livery: ....

Aircraft Weight: .... Height: ....

Aircraft Capacity: .... Wing Shape: ....

Aircraft Length: .... Fuseiage Diameter: ....

Wing Area: .... Based On: ....

Launched In: .... First Flight: ....

✈ Weather ✈

Clean ☐   Sunny ☐   Stormy ☐   Rainy ☐   Cloudy ☐

✈ Equipment Used ✈

✈ Notes ✈

✈ Aircraft Spotted ✈

Date/Time: _____ Where/Location: _____

Airport Details: _____

✈ Aircraft Information ✈

Aircraft Name: _____ Engine Type: _____

Aircraft Model: _____ Engine No: _____

Aircraft Type: _____ Livery: _____

Aircraft Weight: _____ Height: _____

Aircraft Capacity: _____ Wing Shape: _____

Aircraft Length: _____ Fuseiage Diameter: _____

Wing Area: _____ Based On: _____

Launched In: _____ First Flight: _____

✈ Weather ✈

Clean ☐   Sunny ☐   Stormy ☐   Rainy ☐   Cloudy ☐

✈ Equipment Used ✈

_____

_____

_____

✈ Notes ✈

_____

_____

_____

✈ Aircraft Spotted ✈

Date/Time: _____ Where/Location: _____

Airport Details: _____

✈ Aircraft Information ✈

Aircraft Name: _____ Engine Type: _____

Aircraft Model: _____ Engine No: _____

Aircraft Type: _____ Livery: _____

Aircraft Weight: _____ Height: _____

Aircraft Capacity: _____ Wing Shape: _____

Aircraft Length: _____ Fuseiage Diameter: _____

Wing Area: _____ Based On: _____

Launched In: _____ First Flight: _____

✈ Weather ✈

Clean ☐   Sunny ☐   Stormy ☐   Rainy ☐   Cloudy ☐

✈ Equipment Used ✈

_____

_____

_____

✈ Notes ✈

_____

_____

_____

✈ Aircraft Spotted ✈

Date/Time: _____ Where/Location: _____

Airport Details: _____

✈ Aircraft Information ✈

Aircraft Name: _____ Engine Type: _____

Aircraft Model: _____ Engine No: _____

Aircraft Type: _____ Livery: _____

Aircraft Weight: _____ Height: _____

Aircraft Capacity: _____ Wing Shape: _____

Aircraft Length: _____ Fuseiage Diameter: _____

Wing Area: _____ Based On: _____

Launched In: _____ First Flight: _____

✈ Weather ✈

Clean ☐   Sunny ☐   Stormy ☐   Rainy ☐   Cloudy ☐

✈ Equipment Used ✈

_____

_____

_____

✈ Notes ✈

_____

_____

_____

✈ Aircraft Spotted ✈

Date/Time: .... Where/Location: ....

Airport Details: ....

✈ Aircraft Information ✈

Aircraft Name: .... Engine Type: ....

Aircraft Model: .... Engine No: ....

Aircraft Type: .... Livery: ....

Aircraft Weight: .... Height: ....

Aircraft Capacity: .... Wing Shape: ....

Aircraft Length: .... Fuseiage Diameter: ....

Wing Area: .... Based On: ....

Launched In: .... First Flight: ....

✈ Weather ✈

Clean ☐   Sunny ☐   Stormy ☐   Rainy ☐   Cloudy ☐

✈ Equipment Used ✈

✈ Notes ✈

✈ Aircraft Spotted ✈

Date/Time: _____ Where/Location: _____

Airport Details: _____

✈ Aircraft Information ✈

Aircraft Name: _____ Engine Type: _____

Aircraft Model: _____ Engine No: _____

Aircraft Type: _____ Livery: _____

Aircraft Weight: _____ Height: _____

Aircraft Capacity: _____ Wing Shape: _____

Aircraft Length: _____ Fuseiage Diameter: _____

Wing Area: _____ Based On: _____

Launched In: _____ First Flight: _____

✈ Weather ✈

Clean ☐   Sunny ☐   Stormy ☐   Rainy ☐   Cloudy ☐

✈ Equipment Used ✈

_____

_____

_____

✈ Notes ✈

_____

_____

_____

✈ Aircraft Spotted ✈

Date/Time: _ _ _ _ _ _ _ _ _ _ _ _ _ _ _ _ _ Where/Location: _ _ _ _ _ _ _ _ _ _ _ _ _

Airport Details: _

✈ Aircraft Information ✈

Aircraft Name: _ _ _ _ _ _ _ _ _ _ _ _ _ Engine Type: _ _ _ _ _ _ _ _ _ _ _ _ _ _ _

Aircraft Model: _ _ _ _ _ _ _ _ _ _ _ _ Engine No: _ _ _ _ _ _ _ _ _ _ _ _ _ _ _ _

Aircraft Type: _ _ _ _ _ _ _ _ _ _ _ _ _ Livery: _ _ _ _ _ _ _ _ _ _ _ _ _ _ _ _ _ _

Aircraft Weight: _ _ _ _ _ _ _ _ _ _ _ _ Height: _ _ _ _ _ _ _ _ _ _ _ _ _ _ _ _ _ _

Aircraft Capacity: _ _ _ _ _ _ _ _ _ _ _ Wing Shape: _ _ _ _ _ _ _ _ _ _ _ _ _ _ _

Aircraft Length: _ _ _ _ _ _ _ _ _ _ _ _ Fuseiage Diameter: _ _ _ _ _ _ _ _ _ _ _

Wing Area: _ _ _ _ _ _ _ _ _ _ _ _ _ _ _ Based On: _ _ _ _ _ _ _ _ _ _ _ _ _ _ _ _

Launched In: _ _ _ _ _ _ _ _ _ _ _ _ _ _ First Flight: _ _ _ _ _ _ _ _ _ _ _ _ _ _ _

✈ Weather ✈

Clean ☐   Sunny ☐   Stormy ☐   Rainy ☐   Cloudy ☐

✈ Equipment Used ✈

_ _

_ _

_ _

✈ Notes ✈

_ _

_ _

_ _

 Aircraft Spotted

Date/Time:_____ Where/Location:_____

Airport Details:_____

Aircraft Information

Aircraft Name:_____ Engine Type:_____

Aircraft Model:_____ Engine No:_____

Aircraft Type:_____ Livery:_____

Aircraft Weight:_____ Height:_____

Aircraft Capacity:_____ Wing Shape:_____

Aircraft Length:_____ Fuseiage Diameter:_____

Wing Area:_____ Based On:_____

Launched In:_____ First Flight:_____

Weather

Clean ☐   Sunny ☐   Stormy ☐   Rainy ☐   Cloudy ☐

Equipment Used

_____

_____

_____

Notes

_____

_____

_____

✈ Aircraft Spotted ✈

Date/Time: _____ Where/Location: _____

Airport Details: _____

✈ Aircraft Information ✈

Aircraft Name: _____ Engine Type: _____

Aircraft Model: _____ Engine No: _____

Aircraft Type: _____ Livery: _____

Aircraft Weight: _____ Height: _____

Aircraft Capacity: _____ Wing Shape: _____

Aircraft Length: _____ Fuseiage Diameter: _____

Wing Area: _____ Based On: _____

Launched In: _____ First Flight: _____

✈ Weather ✈

Clean ☐   Sunny ☐   Stormy ☐   Rainy ☐   Cloudy ☐

✈ Equipment Used ✈

_____

_____

_____

✈ Notes ✈

_____

_____

_____

✈ Aircraft Spotted ✈

Date/Time: _____ Where/Location: _____

Airport Details: _____

✈ Aircraft Information ✈

Aircraft Name: _____ Engine Type: _____

Aircraft Model: _____ Engine No: _____

Aircraft Type: _____ Livery: _____

Aircraft Weight: _____ Height: _____

Aircraft Capacity: _____ Wing Shape: _____

Aircraft Length: _____ Fuseiage Diameter: _____

Wing Area: _____ Based On: _____

Launched In: _____ First Flight: _____

✈ Weather ✈

Clean ☐   Sunny ☐   Stormy ☐   Rainy ☐   Cloudy ☐

✈ Equipment Used ✈

_____

_____

_____

✈ Notes ✈

_____

_____

_____

✈ Aircraft Spotted ✈

Date/Time: _____ Where/Location: _____

Airport Details: _____

✈ Aircraft Information ✈

Aircraft Name: _____ Engine Type: _____

Aircraft Model: _____ Engine No: _____

Aircraft Type: _____ Livery: _____

Aircraft Weight: _____ Height: _____

Aircraft Capacity: _____ Wing Shape: _____

Aircraft Length: _____ Fuseiage Diameter: _____

Wing Area: _____ Based On: _____

Launched In: _____ First Flight: _____

✈ Weather ✈

Clean ☐   Sunny ☐   Stormy ☐   Rainy ☐   Cloudy ☐

✈ Equipment Used ✈

_____

_____

_____

✈ Notes ✈

_____

_____

_____

✈ Aircraft Spotted ✈

Date/Time: _____ Where/Location: _____

Airport Details: _____

✈ Aircraft Information ✈

Aircraft Name: _____ Engine Type: _____

Aircraft Model: _____ Engine No: _____

Aircraft Type: _____ Livery: _____

Aircraft Weight: _____ Height: _____

Aircraft Capacity: _____ Wing Shape: _____

Aircraft Length: _____ Fuseiage Diameter: _____

Wing Area: _____ Based On: _____

Launched In: _____ First Flight: _____

✈ Weather ✈

Clean ☐   Sunny ☐   Stormy ☐   Rainy ☐   Cloudy ☐

✈ Equipment Used ✈

_____

_____

_____

✈ Notes ✈

_____

_____

_____

 Aircraft Spotted ✈

Date/Time: _____ Where/Location: _____

Airport Details: _____

✈ Aircraft Information ✈

Aircraft Name: _____ Engine Type: _____

Aircraft Model: _____ Engine No: _____

Aircraft Type: _____ Livery: _____

Aircraft Weight: _____ Height: _____

Aircraft Capacity: _____ Wing Shape: _____

Aircraft Length: _____ Fuseiage Diameter: _____

Wing Area: _____ Based On: _____

Launched In: _____ First Flight: _____

✈ Weather ✈

Clean ☐   Sunny ☐   Stormy ☐   Rainy ☐   Cloudy ☐

✈ Equipment Used ✈

_____

_____

_____

✈ Notes ✈

_____

_____

_____

 Aircraft Spotted

Date/Time: _____ Where/Location: _____

Airport Details: _____

Aircraft Information

Aircraft Name: _____ Engine Type: _____

Aircraft Model: _____ Engine No: _____

Aircraft Type: _____ Livery: _____

Aircraft Weight: _____ Height: _____

Aircraft Capacity: _____ Wing Shape: _____

Aircraft Length: _____ Fuseiage Diameter: _____

Wing Area: _____ Based On: _____

Launched In: _____ First Flight: _____

Weather

Clean ☐   Sunny ☐   Stormy ☐   Rainy ☐   Cloudy ☐

Equipment Used

_____

_____

_____

Notes

_____

_____

_____

✈ Aircraft Spotted ✈

Date/Time: _____ Where/Location: _____

Airport Details: _____

✈ Aircraft Information ✈

Aircraft Name: _____ Engine Type: _____

Aircraft Model: _____ Engine No: _____

Aircraft Type: _____ Livery: _____

Aircraft Weight: _____ Height: _____

Aircraft Capacity: _____ Wing Shape: _____

Aircraft Length: _____ Fuseiage Diameter: _____

Wing Area: _____ Based On: _____

Launched In: _____ First Flight: _____

✈ Weather ✈

Clean ☐   Sunny ☐   Stormy ☐   Rainy ☐   Cloudy ☐

✈ Equipment Used ✈

_____

_____

_____

✈ Notes ✈

_____

_____

_____

✈ Aircraft Spotted ✈

Date/Time: _____ Where/Location: _____

Airport Details: _____

✈ Aircraft Information ✈

Aircraft Name: _____ Engine Type: _____

Aircraft Model: _____ Engine No: _____

Aircraft Type: _____ Livery: _____

Aircraft Weight: _____ Height: _____

Aircraft Capacity: _____ Wing Shape: _____

Aircraft Length: _____ Fuseiage Diameter: _____

Wing Area: _____ Based On: _____

Launched In: _____ First Flight: _____

✈ Weather ✈

Clean ☐   Sunny ☐   Stormy ☐   Rainy ☐   Cloudy ☐

✈ Equipment Used ✈

_____

_____

_____

✈ Notes ✈

_____

_____

_____

✈ Aircraft Spotted ✈

Date/Time: _ _ _ _ _ _ _ _ _ _ _ _ _ _ Where/Location: _ _ _ _ _ _ _ _ _ _ _

Airport Details: _

✈ Aircraft Information ✈

Aircraft Name: _ _ _ _ _ _ _ _ _ _ _ _ Engine Type: _ _ _ _ _ _ _ _ _ _ _

Aircraft Model: _ _ _ _ _ _ _ _ _ _ _ Engine No: _ _ _ _ _ _ _ _ _ _ _ _ _

Aircraft Type: _ _ _ _ _ _ _ _ _ _ _ _ Livery: _ _ _ _ _ _ _ _ _ _ _ _ _ _ _

Aircraft Weight: _ _ _ _ _ _ _ _ _ _ Height: _ _ _ _ _ _ _ _ _ _ _ _ _ _ _

Aircraft Capacity: _ _ _ _ _ _ _ _ _ Wing Shape: _ _ _ _ _ _ _ _ _ _ _ _

Aircraft Length: _ _ _ _ _ _ _ _ _ _ Fuseiage Diameter: _ _ _ _ _ _ _ _

Wing Area: _ _ _ _ _ _ _ _ _ _ _ _ _ Based On: _ _ _ _ _ _ _ _ _ _ _ _ _ _

Launched In: _ _ _ _ _ _ _ _ _ _ _ _ First Flight: _ _ _ _ _ _ _ _ _ _ _ _ _

✈ Weather ✈

Clean ☐   Sunny ☐   Stormy ☐   Rainy ☐   Cloudy ☐

✈ Equipment Used ✈

_ _

_ _

_ _

✈ Notes ✈

_ _

_ _

_ _

✈ Aircraft Spotted ✈

Date/Time: _____ Where/Location: _____

Airport Details: _____

✈ Aircraft Information ✈

Aircraft Name: _____ Engine Type: _____

Aircraft Model: _____ Engine No: _____

Aircraft Type: _____ Livery: _____

Aircraft Weight: _____ Height: _____

Aircraft Capacity: _____ Wing Shape: _____

Aircraft Length: _____ Fuseiage Diameter: _____

Wing Area: _____ Based On: _____

Launched In: _____ First Flight: _____

✈ Weather ✈

Clean ☐   Sunny ☐   Stormy ☐   Rainy ☐   Cloudy ☐

✈ Equipment Used ✈

_____

_____

_____

✈ Notes ✈

_____

_____

_____

✈ Aircraft Spotted ✈

Date/Time:........................ Where/Location:...............

Airport Details:..

✈ Aircraft Information ✈

Aircraft Name:.................. Engine Type:..................

Aircraft Model:................. Engine No:....................

Aircraft Type:.................. Livery:.......................

Aircraft Weight:................ Height:.......................

Aircraft Capacity:.............. Wing Shape:...................

Aircraft Length:................ Fuseiage Diameter:............

Wing Area:...................... Based On:.....................

Launched In:.................... First Flight:.................

✈ Weather ✈

Clean ☐   Sunny ☐   Stormy ☐   Rainy ☐   Cloudy ☐

✈ Equipment Used ✈

✈ Notes ✈

 Aircraft Spotted

Date/Time: _____ Where/Location: _____

Airport Details: _____

Aircraft Information

Aircraft Name: _____ Engine Type: _____

Aircraft Model: _____ Engine No: _____

Aircraft Type: _____ Livery: _____

Aircraft Weight: _____ Height: _____

Aircraft Capacity: _____ Wing Shape: _____

Aircraft Length: _____ Fuseiage Diameter: _____

Wing Area: _____ Based On: _____

Launched In: _____ First Flight: _____

Weather

Clean ☐   Sunny ☐   Stormy ☐   Rainy ☐   Cloudy ☐

Equipment Used

_____

_____

_____

Notes

_____

_____

_____

 Aircraft Spotted

Date/Time: _____ Where/Location: _____

Airport Details: _____

Aircraft Information

Aircraft Name: _____ Engine Type: _____

Aircraft Model: _____ Engine No: _____

Aircraft Type: _____ Livery: _____

Aircraft Weight: _____ Height: _____

Aircraft Capacity: _____ Wing Shape: _____

Aircraft Length: _____ Fuseiage Diameter: _____

Wing Area: _____ Based On: _____

Launched In: _____ First Flight: _____

Weather

Clean ☐   Sunny ☐   Stormy ☐   Rainy ☐   Cloudy ☐

Equipment Used

_____

_____

_____

Notes

_____

_____

_____

 Aircraft Spotted ✈

Date/Time: _____ Where/Location: _____

Airport Details: _____

✈ Aircraft Information ✈

Aircraft Name: _____ Engine Type: _____

Aircraft Model: _____ Engine No: _____

Aircraft Type: _____ Livery: _____

Aircraft Weight: _____ Height: _____

Aircraft Capacity: _____ Wing Shape: _____

Aircraft Length: _____ Fuseiage Diameter: _____

Wing Area: _____ Based On: _____

Launched In: _____ First Flight: _____

✈ Weather ✈

Clean ☐   Sunny ☐   Stormy ☐   Rainy ☐   Cloudy ☐

✈ Equipment Used ✈

_____

_____

_____

✈ Notes ✈

_____

_____

_____

✈ Aircraft Spotted ✈

Date/Time: _____ Where/Location: _____

Airport Details: _____

✈ Aircraft Information ✈

Aircraft Name: _____ Engine Type: _____

Aircraft Model: _____ Engine No: _____

Aircraft Type: _____ Livery: _____

Aircraft Weight: _____ Height: _____

Aircraft Capacity: _____ Wing Shape: _____

Aircraft Length: _____ Fuseiage Diameter: _____

Wing Area: _____ Based On: _____

Launched In: _____ First Flight: _____

✈ Weather ✈

Clean ☐   Sunny ☐   Stormy ☐   Rainy ☐   Cloudy ☐

✈ Equipment Used ✈

_____

_____

_____

✈ Notes ✈

_____

_____

_____

✈ Aircraft Spotted ✈

Date/Time: _____ Where/Location: _____

Airport Details: _____

✈ Aircraft Information ✈

Aircraft Name: _____ Engine Type: _____

Aircraft Model: _____ Engine No: _____

Aircraft Type: _____ Livery: _____

Aircraft Weight: _____ Height: _____

Aircraft Capacity: _____ Wing Shape: _____

Aircraft Length: _____ Fuseiage Diameter: _____

Wing Area: _____ Based On: _____

Launched In: _____ First Flight: _____

✈ Weather ✈

Clean ☐   Sunny ☐   Stormy ☐   Rainy ☐   Cloudy ☐

✈ Equipment Used ✈

_____

_____

_____

✈ Notes ✈

_____

_____

_____

✈ Aircraft Spotted ✈

Date/Time: _____ Where/Location: _____

Airport Details: _____

✈ Aircraft Information ✈

Aircraft Name: _____ Engine Type: _____

Aircraft Model: _____ Engine No: _____

Aircraft Type: _____ Livery: _____

Aircraft Weight: _____ Height: _____

Aircraft Capacity: _____ Wing Shape: _____

Aircraft Length: _____ Fuseiage Diameter: _____

Wing Area: _____ Based On: _____

Launched In: _____ First Flight: _____

✈ Weather ✈

Clean ☐   Sunny ☐   Stormy ☐   Rainy ☐   Cloudy ☐

✈ Equipment Used ✈

_____

_____

_____

✈ Notes ✈

_____

_____

_____

 Aircraft Spotted ✈

Date/Time: _____ Where/Location: _____

Airport Details: _____

✈ Aircraft Information ✈

Aircraft Name: _____ Engine Type: _____

Aircraft Model: _____ Engine No: _____

Aircraft Type: _____ Livery: _____

Aircraft Weight: _____ Height: _____

Aircraft Capacity: _____ Wing Shape: _____

Aircraft Length: _____ Fuseiage Diameter: _____

Wing Area: _____ Based On: _____

Launched In: _____ First Flight: _____

✈ Weather ✈

Clean ☐   Sunny ☐   Stormy ☐   Rainy ☐   Cloudy ☐

✈ Equipment Used ✈

_____

_____

_____

✈ Notes ✈

_____

_____

_____

 Aircraft Spotted

Date/Time: _____ Where/Location: _____

Airport Details: _____

Aircraft Information

Aircraft Name: _____ Engine Type: _____

Aircraft Model: _____ Engine No: _____

Aircraft Type: _____ Livery: _____

Aircraft Weight: _____ Height: _____

Aircraft Capacity: _____ Wing Shape: _____

Aircraft Length: _____ Fuseiage Diameter: _____

Wing Area: _____ Based On: _____

Launched In: _____ First Flight: _____

Weather

Clean ☐   Sunny ☐   Stormy ☐   Rainy ☐   Cloudy ☐

Equipment Used

_____

_____

_____

Notes

_____

_____

_____

✈ Aircraft Spotted ✈

Date/Time: _____ Where/Location: _____

Airport Details: _____

✈ Aircraft Information ✈

Aircraft Name: _____ Engine Type: _____

Aircraft Model: _____ Engine No: _____

Aircraft Type: _____ Livery: _____

Aircraft Weight: _____ Height: _____

Aircraft Capacity: _____ Wing Shape: _____

Aircraft Length: _____ Fuseiage Diameter: _____

Wing Area: _____ Based On: _____

Launched In: _____ First Flight: _____

✈ Weather ✈

Clean ☐   Sunny ☐   Stormy ☐   Rainy ☐   Cloudy ☐

✈ Equipment Used ✈

_____

_____

_____

✈ Notes ✈

_____

_____

_____

✈ Aircraft Spotted ✈

Date/Time: _____ Where/Location: _____

Airport Details: _____

✈ Aircraft Information ✈

Aircraft Name: _____ Engine Type: _____

Aircraft Model: _____ Engine No: _____

Aircraft Type: _____ Livery: _____

Aircraft Weight: _____ Height: _____

Aircraft Capacity: _____ Wing Shape: _____

Aircraft Length: _____ Fuseiage Diameter: _____

Wing Area: _____ Based On: _____

Launched In: _____ First Flight: _____

✈ Weather ✈

Clean ☐   Sunny ☐   Stormy ☐   Rainy ☐   Cloudy ☐

✈ Equipment Used ✈

✈ Notes ✈

✈ Aircraft Spotted ✈

Date/Time: _____ Where/Location: _____

Airport Details: _____

✈ Aircraft Information ✈

Aircraft Name: _____ Engine Type: _____

Aircraft Model: _____ Engine No: _____

Aircraft Type: _____ Livery: _____

Aircraft Weight: _____ Height: _____

Aircraft Capacity: _____ Wing Shape: _____

Aircraft Length: _____ Fuseiage Diameter: _____

Wing Area: _____ Based On: _____

Launched In: _____ First Flight: _____

✈ Weather ✈

Clean ☐   Sunny ☐   Stormy ☐   Rainy ☐   Cloudy ☐

✈ Equipment Used ✈

_____

_____

_____

✈ Notes ✈

_____

_____

_____

✈ Aircraft Spotted ✈

Date/Time: _____ Where/Location: _____

Airport Details: _____

✈ Aircraft Information ✈

Aircraft Name: _____ Engine Type: _____

Aircraft Model: _____ Engine No: _____

Aircraft Type: _____ Livery: _____

Aircraft Weight: _____ Height: _____

Aircraft Capacity: _____ Wing Shape: _____

Aircraft Length: _____ Fuseiage Diameter: _____

Wing Area: _____ Based On: _____

Launched In: _____ First Flight: _____

✈ Weather ✈

Clean ☐   Sunny ☐   Stormy ☐   Rainy ☐   Cloudy ☐

✈ Equipment Used ✈

_____

_____

_____

✈ Notes ✈

_____

_____

_____

 Aircraft Spotted

Date/Time: _____ Where/Location: _____

Airport Details: _____

✈ Aircraft Information ✈

Aircraft Name: _____ Engine Type: _____

Aircraft Model: _____ Engine No: _____

Aircraft Type: _____ Livery: _____

Aircraft Weight: _____ Height: _____

Aircraft Capacity: _____ Wing Shape: _____

Aircraft Length: _____ Fuseiage Diameter: _____

Wing Area: _____ Based On: _____

Launched In: _____ First Flight: _____

✈ Weather ✈

Clean ☐   Sunny ☐   Stormy ☐   Rainy ☐   Cloudy ☐

✈ Equipment Used ✈

_____

_____

_____

✈ Notes ✈

_____

_____

_____

✈ Aircraft Spotted ✈

Date/Time: _____ Where/Location: _____

Airport Details: _____

✈ Aircraft Information ✈

Aircraft Name: _____ Engine Type: _____

Aircraft Model: _____ Engine No: _____

Aircraft Type: _____ Livery: _____

Aircraft Weight: _____ Height: _____

Aircraft Capacity: _____ Wing Shape: _____

Aircraft Length: _____ Fuseiage Diameter: _____

Wing Area: _____ Based On: _____

Launched In: _____ First Flight: _____

✈ Weather ✈

Clean ☐   Sunny ☐   Stormy ☐   Rainy ☐   Cloudy ☐

✈ Equipment Used ✈

_____

_____

_____

✈ Notes ✈

_____

_____

_____

✈ Aircraft Spotted ✈

Date/Time: _____ Where/Location: _____

Airport Details: _____

✈ Aircraft Information ✈

Aircraft Name: _____ Engine Type: _____

Aircraft Model: _____ Engine No: _____

Aircraft Type: _____ Livery: _____

Aircraft Weight: _____ Height: _____

Aircraft Capacity: _____ Wing Shape: _____

Aircraft Length: _____ Fuseiage Diameter: _____

Wing Area: _____ Based On: _____

Launched In: _____ First Flight: _____

✈ Weather ✈

Clean ☐   Sunny ☐   Stormy ☐   Rainy ☐   Cloudy ☐

✈ Equipment Used ✈

✈ Notes ✈

✈ Aircraft Spotted ✈

Date/Time: _____ Where/Location: _____

Airport Details: _____

✈ Aircraft Information ✈

Aircraft Name: _____ Engine Type: _____

Aircraft Model: _____ Engine No: _____

Aircraft Type: _____ Livery: _____

Aircraft Weight: _____ Height: _____

Aircraft Capacity: _____ Wing Shape: _____

Aircraft Length: _____ Fuseiage Diameter: _____

Wing Area: _____ Based On: _____

Launched In: _____ First Flight: _____

✈ Weather ✈

Clean ☐   Sunny ☐   Stormy ☐   Rainy ☐   Cloudy ☐

✈ Equipment Used ✈

_____

_____

_____

✈ Notes ✈

_____

_____

_____

✈ Aircraft Spotted ✈

Date/Time: _____ Where/Location: _____

Airport Details: _____

✈ Aircraft Information ✈

Aircraft Name: _____ Engine Type: _____

Aircraft Model: _____ Engine No: _____

Aircraft Type: _____ Livery: _____

Aircraft Weight: _____ Height: _____

Aircraft Capacity: _____ Wing Shape: _____

Aircraft Length: _____ Fuseiage Diameter: _____

Wing Area: _____ Based On: _____

Launched In: _____ First Flight: _____

✈ Weather ✈

Clean ☐   Sunny ☐   Stormy ☐   Rainy ☐   Cloudy ☐

✈ Equipment Used ✈

_____

_____

_____

✈ Notes ✈

_____

_____

_____

 Aircraft Spotted

Date/Time: _____ Where/Location: _____

Airport Details: _____

Aircraft Information

Aircraft Name: _____ Engine Type: _____

Aircraft Model: _____ Engine No: _____

Aircraft Type: _____ Livery: _____

Aircraft Weight: _____ Height: _____

Aircraft Capacity: _____ Wing Shape: _____

Aircraft Length: _____ Fuseiage Diameter: _____

Wing Area: _____ Based On: _____

Launched In: _____ First Flight: _____

Weather

Clean ☐   Sunny ☐   Stormy ☐   Rainy ☐   Cloudy ☐

Equipment Used

_____

_____

_____

Notes

_____

_____

_____

✈ Aircraft Spotted ✈

Date/Time: _____ Where/Location: _____

Airport Details: _____

✈ Aircraft Information ✈

Aircraft Name: _____ Engine Type: _____

Aircraft Model: _____ Engine No: _____

Aircraft Type: _____ Livery: _____

Aircraft Weight: _____ Height: _____

Aircraft Capacity: _____ Wing Shape: _____

Aircraft Length: _____ Fuseiage Diameter: _____

Wing Area: _____ Based On: _____

Launched In: _____ First Flight: _____

✈ Weather ✈

Clean ☐   Sunny ☐   Stormy ☐   Rainy ☐   Cloudy ☐

✈ Equipment Used ✈

_____

_____

_____

✈ Notes ✈

_____

_____

_____

✈ Aircraft Spotted ✈

Date/Time: _____ Where/Location: _____

Airport Details: _____

✈ Aircraft Information ✈

Aircraft Name: _____ Engine Type: _____

Aircraft Model: _____ Engine No: _____

Aircraft Type: _____ Livery: _____

Aircraft Weight: _____ Height: _____

Aircraft Capacity: _____ Wing Shape: _____

Aircraft Length: _____ Fuseiage Diameter: _____

Wing Area: _____ Based On: _____

Launched In: _____ First Flight: _____

✈ Weather ✈

Clean ☐   Sunny ☐   Stormy ☐   Rainy ☐   Cloudy ☐

✈ Equipment Used ✈

_____

_____

_____

✈ Notes ✈

_____

_____

_____

✈ Aircraft Spotted ✈

Date/Time: _____ Where/Location: _____

Airport Details: _____

✈ Aircraft Information ✈

Aircraft Name: _____ Engine Type: _____

Aircraft Model: _____ Engine No: _____

Aircraft Type: _____ Livery: _____

Aircraft Weight: _____ Height: _____

Aircraft Capacity: _____ Wing Shape: _____

Aircraft Length: _____ Fuseiage Diameter: _____

Wing Area: _____ Based On: _____

Launched In: _____ First Flight: _____

✈ Weather ✈

Clean ☐   Sunny ☐   Stormy ☐   Rainy ☐   Cloudy ☐

✈ Equipment Used ✈

_____

_____

_____

✈ Notes ✈

_____

_____

_____

✈ Aircraft Spotted ✈

Date/Time: _____ Where/Location: _____

Airport Details: _____

✈ Aircraft Information ✈

Aircraft Name: _____ Engine Type: _____

Aircraft Model: _____ Engine No: _____

Aircraft Type: _____ Livery: _____

Aircraft Weight: _____ Height: _____

Aircraft Capacity: _____ Wing Shape: _____

Aircraft Length: _____ Fuseiage Diameter: _____

Wing Area: _____ Based On: _____

Launched In: _____ First Flight: _____

✈ Weather ✈

Clean ☐   Sunny ☐   Stormy ☐   Rainy ☐   Cloudy ☐

✈ Equipment Used ✈

_____

_____

_____

✈ Notes ✈

_____

_____

_____

 Aircraft Spotted ✈

Date/Time: _____ Where/Location: _____

Airport Details: _____

✈ Aircraft Information ✈

Aircraft Name: _____ Engine Type: _____

Aircraft Model: _____ Engine No: _____

Aircraft Type: _____ Livery: _____

Aircraft Weight: _____ Height: _____

Aircraft Capacity: _____ Wing Shape: _____

Aircraft Length: _____ Fuseiage Diameter: _____

Wing Area: _____ Based On: _____

Launched In: _____ First Flight: _____

✈ Weather ✈

Clean ☐   Sunny ☐   Stormy ☐   Rainy ☐   Cloudy ☐

✈ Equipment Used ✈

_____

_____

_____

✈ Notes ✈

_____

_____

_____

 Aircraft Spotted ✈

Date/Time: _____ Where/Location: _____

Airport Details: _____

✈ Aircraft Information ✈

Aircraft Name: _____ Engine Type: _____

Aircraft Model: _____ Engine No: _____

Aircraft Type: _____ Livery: _____

Aircraft Weight: _____ Height: _____

Aircraft Capacity: _____ Wing Shape: _____

Aircraft Length: _____ Fuseiage Diameter: _____

Wing Area: _____ Based On: _____

Launched In: _____ First Flight: _____

✈ Weather ✈

Clean ☐   Sunny ☐   Stormy ☐   Rainy ☐   Cloudy ☐

✈ Equipment Used ✈

_____

_____

_____

✈ Notes ✈

_____

_____

_____

✈ Aircraft Spotted ✈

Date/Time: _____ Where/Location: _____

Airport Details: _____

✈ Aircraft Information ✈

Aircraft Name: _____ Engine Type: _____

Aircraft Model: _____ Engine No: _____

Aircraft Type: _____ Livery: _____

Aircraft Weight: _____ Height: _____

Aircraft Capacity: _____ Wing Shape: _____

Aircraft Length: _____ Fuseiage Diameter: _____

Wing Area: _____ Based On: _____

Launched In: _____ First Flight: _____

✈ Weather ✈

Clean ☐   Sunny ☐   Stormy ☐   Rainy ☐   Cloudy ☐

✈ Equipment Used ✈

_____

_____

_____

✈ Notes ✈

_____

_____

_____

✈ Aircraft Spotted ✈

Date/Time: _____ Where/Location: _____

Airport Details: _____

✈ Aircraft Information ✈

Aircraft Name: _____ Engine Type: _____

Aircraft Model: _____ Engine No: _____

Aircraft Type: _____ Livery: _____

Aircraft Weight: _____ Height: _____

Aircraft Capacity: _____ Wing Shape: _____

Aircraft Length: _____ Fuseiage Diameter: _____

Wing Area: _____ Based On: _____

Launched In: _____ First Flight: _____

✈ Weather ✈

Clean ☐   Sunny ☐   Stormy ☐   Rainy ☐   Cloudy ☐

✈ Equipment Used ✈

_____

_____

_____

✈ Notes ✈

_____

_____

_____

✈ Aircraft Spotted ✈

Date/Time: _____ Where/Location: _____

Airport Details: _____

✈ Aircraft Information ✈

Aircraft Name: _____ Engine Type: _____

Aircraft Model: _____ Engine No: _____

Aircraft Type: _____ Livery: _____

Aircraft Weight: _____ Height: _____

Aircraft Capacity: _____ Wing Shape: _____

Aircraft Length: _____ Fuseiage Diameter: _____

Wing Area: _____ Based On: _____

Launched In: _____ First Flight: _____

✈ Weather ✈

Clean ☐   Sunny ☐   Stormy ☐   Rainy ☐   Cloudy ☐

✈ Equipment Used ✈

_____

_____

_____

✈ Notes ✈

_____

_____

_____

✈ Aircraft Spotted ✈

Date/Time: _____ Where/Location: _____

Airport Details: _____

✈ Aircraft Information ✈

Aircraft Name: _____ Engine Type: _____

Aircraft Model: _____ Engine No: _____

Aircraft Type: _____ Livery: _____

Aircraft Weight: _____ Height: _____

Aircraft Capacity: _____ Wing Shape: _____

Aircraft Length: _____ Fuseiage Diameter: _____

Wing Area: _____ Based On: _____

Launched In: _____ First Flight: _____

✈ Weather ✈

Clean ☐   Sunny ☐   Stormy ☐   Rainy ☐   Cloudy ☐

✈ Equipment Used ✈

_____

_____

_____

✈ Notes ✈

_____

_____

_____

✈ Aircraft Spotted ✈

Date/Time: _____ Where/Location: _____

Airport Details: _____

✈ Aircraft Information ✈

Aircraft Name: _____ Engine Type: _____

Aircraft Model: _____ Engine No: _____

Aircraft Type: _____ Livery: _____

Aircraft Weight: _____ Height: _____

Aircraft Capacity: _____ Wing Shape: _____

Aircraft Length: _____ Fuseiage Diameter: _____

Wing Area: _____ Based On: _____

Launched In: _____ First Flight: _____

✈ Weather ✈

Clean ☐   Sunny ☐   Stormy ☐   Rainy ☐   Cloudy ☐

✈ Equipment Used ✈

_____

_____

_____

✈ Notes ✈

_____

_____

_____

 Aircraft Spotted ✈

Date/Time: _____ Where/Location: _____

Airport Details: _____

✈ Aircraft Information ✈

Aircraft Name: _____ Engine Type: _____

Aircraft Model: _____ Engine No: _____

Aircraft Type: _____ Livery: _____

Aircraft Weight: _____ Height: _____

Aircraft Capacity: _____ Wing Shape: _____

Aircraft Length: _____ Fuseiage Diameter: _____

Wing Area: _____ Based On: _____

Launched In: _____ First Flight: _____

✈ Weather ✈

Clean ☐   Sunny ☐   Stormy ☐   Rainy ☐   Cloudy ☐

✈ Equipment Used ✈

_____

_____

_____

✈ Notes ✈

_____

_____

_____

✈ Aircraft Spotted ✈

Date/Time: _____ Where/Location: _____

Airport Details: _____

✈ Aircraft Information ✈

Aircraft Name: _____ Engine Type: _____

Aircraft Model: _____ Engine No: _____

Aircraft Type: _____ Livery: _____

Aircraft Weight: _____ Height: _____

Aircraft Capacity: _____ Wing Shape: _____

Aircraft Length: _____ Fuseiage Diameter: _____

Wing Area: _____ Based On: _____

Launched In: _____ First Flight: _____

✈ Weather ✈

Clean ☐   Sunny ☐   Stormy ☐   Rainy ☐   Cloudy ☐

✈ Equipment Used ✈

_____

_____

_____

✈ Notes ✈

_____

_____

_____

✈ Aircraft Spotted ✈

Date/Time: _____ Where/Location: _____

Airport Details: _____

✈ Aircraft Information ✈

Aircraft Name: _____ Engine Type: _____

Aircraft Model: _____ Engine No: _____

Aircraft Type: _____ Livery: _____

Aircraft Weight: _____ Height: _____

Aircraft Capacity: _____ Wing Shape: _____

Aircraft Length: _____ Fuseiage Diameter: _____

Wing Area: _____ Based On: _____

Launched In: _____ First Flight: _____

✈ Weather ✈

Clean ☐   Sunny ☐   Stormy ☐   Rainy ☐   Cloudy ☐

✈ Equipment Used ✈

✈ Notes ✈

✈ Aircraft Spotted ✈

Date/Time: _____ Where/Location: _____

Airport Details: _____

✈ Aircraft Information ✈

Aircraft Name: _____ Engine Type: _____

Aircraft Model: _____ Engine No: _____

Aircraft Type: _____ Livery: _____

Aircraft Weight: _____ Height: _____

Aircraft Capacity: _____ Wing Shape: _____

Aircraft Length: _____ Fuseiage Diameter: _____

Wing Area: _____ Based On: _____

Launched In: _____ First Flight: _____

✈ Weather ✈

Clean ☐   Sunny ☐   Stormy ☐   Rainy ☐   Cloudy ☐

✈ Equipment Used ✈

_____

_____

_____

✈ Notes ✈

_____

_____

_____

✈ Aircraft Spotted ✈

Date/Time: _ _ _ _ _ _ _ _ _ _ _ Where/Location: _ _ _ _ _ _ _ _

Airport Details: _

✈ Aircraft Information ✈

Aircraft Name: _ _ _ _ _ _ _ _ _ Engine Type: _ _ _ _ _ _ _ _

Aircraft Model: _ _ _ _ _ _ _ _ _ Engine No: _ _ _ _ _ _ _ _ _

Aircraft Type: _ _ _ _ _ _ _ _ _ _ Livery: _ _ _ _ _ _ _ _ _ _ _

Aircraft Weight: _ _ _ _ _ _ _ _ _ Height: _ _ _ _ _ _ _ _ _ _ _

Aircraft Capacity: _ _ _ _ _ _ _ _ Wing Shape: _ _ _ _ _ _ _ _

Aircraft Length: _ _ _ _ _ _ _ _ _ Fuseiage Diameter: _ _ _ _ _

Wing Area: _ _ _ _ _ _ _ _ _ _ _ _ Based On: _ _ _ _ _ _ _ _ _

Launched In: _ _ _ _ _ _ _ _ _ _ _ First Flight: _ _ _ _ _ _ _ _ _

✈ Weather ✈

Clean ☐   Sunny ☐   Stormy ☐   Rainy ☐   Cloudy ☐

✈ Equipment Used ✈

_ _

_ _

_ _

✈ Notes ✈

_ _

_ _

_ _

✈ Aircraft Spotted ✈

Date/Time: _____ Where/Location: _____

Airport Details: _____

✈ Aircraft Information ✈

Aircraft Name: _____ Engine Type: _____

Aircraft Model: _____ Engine No: _____

Aircraft Type: _____ Livery: _____

Aircraft Weight: _____ Height: _____

Aircraft Capacity: _____ Wing Shape: _____

Aircraft Length: _____ Fuseiage Diameter: _____

Wing Area: _____ Based On: _____

Launched In: _____ First Flight: _____

✈ Weather ✈

Clean ☐   Sunny ☐   Stormy ☐   Rainy ☐   Cloudy ☐

✈ Equipment Used ✈

_____

_____

_____

✈ Notes ✈

_____

_____

_____

✈ Aircraft Spotted ✈

Date/Time: _____ Where/Location: _____

Airport Details: _____

✈ Aircraft Information ✈

Aircraft Name: _____ Engine Type: _____

Aircraft Model: _____ Engine No: _____

Aircraft Type: _____ Livery: _____

Aircraft Weight: _____ Height: _____

Aircraft Capacity: _____ Wing Shape: _____

Aircraft Length: _____ Fuseiage Diameter: _____

Wing Area: _____ Based On: _____

Launched In: _____ First Flight: _____

✈ Weather ✈

Clean ☐   Sunny ☐   Stormy ☐   Rainy ☐   Cloudy ☐

✈ Equipment Used ✈

_____

_____

_____

✈ Notes ✈

_____

_____

_____

 Aircraft Spotted

Date/Time:................................ Where/Location:...................

Airport Details:..

Aircraft Information

Aircraft Name:....................... Engine Type:....................

Aircraft Model:...................... Engine No:......................

Aircraft Type:....................... Livery:.........................

Aircraft Weight:..................... Height:.........................

Aircraft Capacity:................... Wing Shape:.....................

Aircraft Length:..................... Fuseiage Diameter:..............

Wing Area:........................... Based On:.......................

Launched In:......................... First Flight:...................

Weather

Clean ☐   Sunny ☐   Stormy ☐   Rainy ☐   Cloudy ☐

Equipment Used

....

....

....

Notes

....

....

....

✈ Aircraft Spotted ✈

Date/Time: _____ Where/Location: _____

Airport Details: _____

✈ Aircraft Information ✈

Aircraft Name: _____ Engine Type: _____

Aircraft Model: _____ Engine No: _____

Aircraft Type: _____ Livery: _____

Aircraft Weight: _____ Height: _____

Aircraft Capacity: _____ Wing Shape: _____

Aircraft Length: _____ Fuseiage Diameter: _____

Wing Area: _____ Based On: _____

Launched In: _____ First Flight: _____

✈ Weather ✈

Clean ☐   Sunny ☐   Stormy ☐   Rainy ☐   Cloudy ☐

✈ Equipment Used ✈

_____

_____

_____

✈ Notes ✈

_____

_____

_____

✈ Aircraft Spotted ✈

Date/Time: _____ Where/Location: _____

Airport Details: _____

✈ Aircraft Information ✈

Aircraft Name: _____ Engine Type: _____

Aircraft Model: _____ Engine No: _____

Aircraft Type: _____ Livery: _____

Aircraft Weight: _____ Height: _____

Aircraft Capacity: _____ Wing Shape: _____

Aircraft Length: _____ Fuseiage Diameter: _____

Wing Area: _____ Based On: _____

Launched In: _____ First Flight: _____

✈ Weather ✈

Clean ☐   Sunny ☐   Stormy ☐   Rainy ☐   Cloudy ☐

✈ Equipment Used ✈

_____

_____

_____

✈ Notes ✈

_____

_____

_____

✈ Aircraft Spotted ✈

Date/Time: _____ Where/Location: _____

Airport Details: _____

✈ Aircraft Information ✈

Aircraft Name: _____ Engine Type: _____

Aircraft Model: _____ Engine No: _____

Aircraft Type: _____ Livery: _____

Aircraft Weight: _____ Height: _____

Aircraft Capacity: _____ Wing Shape: _____

Aircraft Length: _____ Fuseiage Diameter: _____

Wing Area: _____ Based On: _____

Launched In: _____ First Flight: _____

✈ Weather ✈

Clean ☐   Sunny ☐   Stormy ☐   Rainy ☐   Cloudy ☐

✈ Equipment Used ✈

_____

_____

_____

✈ Notes ✈

_____

_____

_____

✈ Aircraft Spotted ✈

Date/Time: _____ Where/Location: _____

Airport Details: _____

✈ Aircraft Information ✈

Aircraft Name: _____ Engine Type: _____

Aircraft Model: _____ Engine No: _____

Aircraft Type: _____ Livery: _____

Aircraft Weight: _____ Height: _____

Aircraft Capacity: _____ Wing Shape: _____

Aircraft Length: _____ Fuseiage Diameter: _____

Wing Area: _____ Based On: _____

Launched In: _____ First Flight: _____

✈ Weather ✈

Clean ☐   Sunny ☐   Stormy ☐   Rainy ☐   Cloudy ☐

✈ Equipment Used ✈

_____

_____

_____

✈ Notes ✈

_____

_____

_____

✈ Aircraft Spotted ✈

Date/Time: _____ Where/Location: _____

Airport Details: _____

✈ Aircraft Information ✈

Aircraft Name: _____ Engine Type: _____

Aircraft Model: _____ Engine No: _____

Aircraft Type: _____ Livery: _____

Aircraft Weight: _____ Height: _____

Aircraft Capacity: _____ Wing Shape: _____

Aircraft Length: _____ Fuseiage Diameter: _____

Wing Area: _____ Based On: _____

Launched In: _____ First Flight: _____

✈ Weather ✈

Clean ☐   Sunny ☐   Stormy ☐   Rainy ☐   Cloudy ☐

✈ Equipment Used ✈

_____

_____

_____

✈ Notes ✈

_____

_____

_____

✈ Aircraft Spotted ✈

Date/Time: _____ Where/Location: _____

Airport Details: _____

✈ Aircraft Information ✈

Aircraft Name: _____ Engine Type: _____

Aircraft Model: _____ Engine No: _____

Aircraft Type: _____ Livery: _____

Aircraft Weight: _____ Height: _____

Aircraft Capacity: _____ Wing Shape: _____

Aircraft Length: _____ Fuseiage Diameter: _____

Wing Area: _____ Based On: _____

Launched In: _____ First Flight: _____

✈ Weather ✈

Clean ☐   Sunny ☐   Stormy ☐   Rainy ☐   Cloudy ☐

✈ Equipment Used ✈

_____

_____

_____

✈ Notes ✈

_____

_____

_____

✈ Aircraft Spotted ✈

Date/Time: _____ Where/Location: _____

Airport Details: _____

✈ Aircraft Information ✈

Aircraft Name: _____ Engine Type: _____

Aircraft Model: _____ Engine No: _____

Aircraft Type: _____ Livery: _____

Aircraft Weight: _____ Height: _____

Aircraft Capacity: _____ Wing Shape: _____

Aircraft Length: _____ Fuseiage Diameter: ___

Wing Area: _____ Based On: _____

Launched In: _____ First Flight: _____

✈ Weather ✈

Clean ☐   Sunny ☐   Stormy ☐   Rainy ☐   Cloudy ☐

✈ Equipment Used ✈

✈ Notes ✈

✈ Aircraft Spotted ✈

Date/Time: _____ Where/Location: _____

Airport Details: _____

✈ Aircraft Information ✈

Aircraft Name: _____ Engine Type: _____

Aircraft Model: _____ Engine No: _____

Aircraft Type: _____ Livery: _____

Aircraft Weight: _____ Height: _____

Aircraft Capacity: _____ Wing Shape: _____

Aircraft Length: _____ Fuseiage Diameter: _____

Wing Area: _____ Based On: _____

Launched In: _____ First Flight: _____

✈ Weather ✈

Clean ☐   Sunny ☐   Stormy ☐   Rainy ☐   Cloudy ☐

✈ Equipment Used ✈

_____

_____

_____

✈ Notes ✈

_____

_____

_____

✈ Aircraft Spotted ✈

Date/Time: _____ Where/Location: _____

Airport Details: _____

✈ Aircraft Information ✈

Aircraft Name: _____ Engine Type: _____

Aircraft Model: _____ Engine No: _____

Aircraft Type: _____ Livery: _____

Aircraft Weight: _____ Height: _____

Aircraft Capacity: _____ Wing Shape: _____

Aircraft Length: _____ Fuseiage Diameter: _____

Wing Area: _____ Based On: _____

Launched In: _____ First Flight: _____

✈ Weather ✈

Clean ☐   Sunny ☐   Stormy ☐   Rainy ☐   Cloudy ☐

✈ Equipment Used ✈

_____

_____

_____

✈ Notes ✈

_____

_____

_____

✈ Aircraft Spotted ✈

Date/Time: _____ Where/Location: _____

Airport Details: _____

✈ Aircraft Information ✈

Aircraft Name: _____ Engine Type: _____

Aircraft Model: _____ Engine No: _____

Aircraft Type: _____ Livery: _____

Aircraft Weight: _____ Height: _____

Aircraft Capacity: _____ Wing Shape: _____

Aircraft Length: _____ Fuseiage Diameter: _____

Wing Area: _____ Based On: _____

Launched In: _____ First Flight: _____

✈ Weather ✈

Clean ☐   Sunny ☐   Stormy ☐   Rainy ☐   Cloudy ☐

✈ Equipment Used ✈

_____

_____

_____

✈ Notes ✈

_____

_____

_____

✈ Aircraft Spotted ✈

Date/Time: _____ Where/Location: _____

Airport Details: _____

✈ Aircraft Information ✈

Aircraft Name: _____ Engine Type: _____

Aircraft Model: _____ Engine No: _____

Aircraft Type: _____ Livery: _____

Aircraft Weight: _____ Height: _____

Aircraft Capacity: _____ Wing Shape: _____

Aircraft Length: _____ Fuseiage Diameter: _____

Wing Area: _____ Based On: _____

Launched In: _____ First Flight: _____

✈ Weather ✈

Clean ☐   Sunny ☐   Stormy ☐   Rainy ☐   Cloudy ☐

✈ Equipment Used ✈

_____

_____

_____

✈ Notes ✈

_____

_____

_____

✈ Aircraft Spotted ✈

Date/Time: _____ Where/Location: _____

Airport Details: _____

✈ Aircraft Information ✈

Aircraft Name: _____ Engine Type: _____

Aircraft Model: _____ Engine No: _____

Aircraft Type: _____ Livery: _____

Aircraft Weight: _____ Height: _____

Aircraft Capacity: _____ Wing Shape: _____

Aircraft Length: _____ Fuseiage Diameter: _____

Wing Area: _____ Based On: _____

Launched In: _____ First Flight: _____

✈ Weather ✈

Clean ☐   Sunny ☐   Stormy ☐   Rainy ☐   Cloudy ☐

✈ Equipment Used ✈

_____

_____

_____

✈ Notes ✈

_____

_____

_____

✈ Aircraft Spotted ✈

Date/Time: _____ Where/Location: _____

Airport Details: _____

✈ Aircraft Information ✈

Aircraft Name: _____ Engine Type: _____

Aircraft Model: _____ Engine No: _____

Aircraft Type: _____ Livery: _____

Aircraft Weight: _____ Height: _____

Aircraft Capacity: _____ Wing Shape: _____

Aircraft Length: _____ Fuseiage Diameter: _____

Wing Area: _____ Based On: _____

Launched In: _____ First Flight: _____

✈ Weather ✈

Clean ☐   Sunny ☐   Stormy ☐   Rainy ☐   Cloudy ☐

✈ Equipment Used ✈

_____

_____

_____

✈ Notes ✈

_____

_____

_____

✈ Aircraft Spotted ✈

Date/Time: _____ Where/Location: _____

Airport Details: _____

✈ Aircraft Information ✈

Aircraft Name: _____ Engine Type: _____

Aircraft Model: _____ Engine No: _____

Aircraft Type: _____ Livery: _____

Aircraft Weight: _____ Height: _____

Aircraft Capacity: _____ Wing Shape: _____

Aircraft Length: _____ Fuseiage Diameter: _____

Wing Area: _____ Based On: _____

Launched In: _____ First Flight: _____

✈ Weather ✈

Clean ☐   Sunny ☐   Stormy ☐   Rainy ☐   Cloudy ☐

✈ Equipment Used ✈

_____

_____

_____

✈ Notes ✈

_____

_____

_____

✈ Aircraft Spotted ✈

Date/Time:_____ Where/Location:_____

Airport Details:_____

✈ Aircraft Information ✈

Aircraft Name:_____ Engine Type:_____

Aircraft Model:_____ Engine No:_____

Aircraft Type:_____ Livery:_____

Aircraft Weight:_____ Height:_____

Aircraft Capacity:_____ Wing Shape:_____

Aircraft Length:_____ Fuseiage Diameter:_____

Wing Area:_____ Based On:_____

Launched In:_____ First Flight:_____

✈ Weather ✈

Clean ☐   Sunny ☐   Stormy ☐   Rainy ☐   Cloudy ☐

✈ Equipment Used ✈

_____

_____

_____

✈ Notes ✈

_____

_____

_____

 Aircraft Spotted ✈

Date/Time: _____ Where/Location: _____

Airport Details: _____

✈ Aircraft Information ✈

Aircraft Name: _____ Engine Type: _____

Aircraft Model: _____ Engine No: _____

Aircraft Type: _____ Livery: _____

Aircraft Weight: _____ Height: _____

Aircraft Capacity: _____ Wing Shape: _____

Aircraft Length: _____ Fuseiage Diameter: _____

Wing Area: _____ Based On: _____

Launched In: _____ First Flight: _____

✈ Weather ✈

Clean ☐   Sunny ☐   Stormy ☐   Rainy ☐   Cloudy ☐

✈ Equipment Used ✈

_____

_____

_____

✈ Notes ✈

_____

_____

_____

✈ Aircraft Spotted ✈

Date/Time: _____ Where/Location: _____

Airport Details: _____

✈ Aircraft Information ✈

Aircraft Name: _____ Engine Type: _____

Aircraft Model: _____ Engine No: _____

Aircraft Type: _____ Livery: _____

Aircraft Weight: _____ Height: _____

Aircraft Capacity: _____ Wing Shape: _____

Aircraft Length: _____ Fuseiage Diameter: _____

Wing Area: _____ Based On: _____

Launched In: _____ First Flight: _____

✈ Weather ✈

Clean ☐   Sunny ☐   Stormy ☐   Rainy ☐   Cloudy ☐

✈ Equipment Used ✈

_____

_____

_____

✈ Notes ✈

_____

_____

_____

✈ Aircraft Spotted ✈

Date/Time:_____ Where/Location:_____

Airport Details:_____

✈ Aircraft Information ✈

Aircraft Name:_____ Engine Type:_____

Aircraft Model:_____ Engine No:_____

Aircraft Type:_____ Livery:_____

Aircraft Weight:_____ Height:_____

Aircraft Capacity:_____ Wing Shape:_____

Aircraft Length:_____ Fuseiage Diameter:_____

Wing Area:_____ Based On:_____

Launched In:_____ First Flight:_____

✈ Weather ✈

Clean ☐   Sunny ☐   Stormy ☐   Rainy ☐   Cloudy ☐

✈ Equipment Used ✈

_____

_____

_____

✈ Notes ✈

_____

_____

_____

✈ Aircraft Spotted ✈

Date/Time: _____ Where/Location: _____

Airport Details: _____

✈ Aircraft Information ✈

Aircraft Name: _____ Engine Type: _____

Aircraft Model: _____ Engine No: _____

Aircraft Type: _____ Livery: _____

Aircraft Weight: _____ Height: _____

Aircraft Capacity: _____ Wing Shape: _____

Aircraft Length: _____ Fuseiage Diameter: _____

Wing Area: _____ Based On: _____

Launched In: _____ First Flight: _____

✈ Weather ✈

Clean ☐   Sunny ☐   Stormy ☐   Rainy ☐   Cloudy ☐

✈ Equipment Used ✈

_____

_____

_____

✈ Notes ✈

_____

_____

_____

✈ Aircraft Spotted ✈

Date/Time: _____ Where/Location: _____

Airport Details: _____

✈ Aircraft Information ✈

Aircraft Name: _____ Engine Type: _____

Aircraft Model: _____ Engine No: _____

Aircraft Type: _____ Livery: _____

Aircraft Weight: _____ Height: _____

Aircraft Capacity: _____ Wing Shape: _____

Aircraft Length: _____ Fuseiage Diameter: _____

Wing Area: _____ Based On: _____

Launched In: _____ First Flight: _____

✈ Weather ✈

Clean ☐   Sunny ☐   Stormy ☐   Rainy ☐   Cloudy ☐

✈ Equipment Used ✈

_____

_____

_____

✈ Notes ✈

_____

_____

_____

✈ Aircraft Spotted ✈

Date/Time: _____ Where/Location: _____

Airport Details: _____

✈ Aircraft Information ✈

Aircraft Name: _____ Engine Type: _____

Aircraft Model: _____ Engine No: _____

Aircraft Type: _____ Livery: _____

Aircraft Weight: _____ Height: _____

Aircraft Capacity: _____ Wing Shape: _____

Aircraft Length: _____ Fuseiage Diameter: _____

Wing Area: _____ Based On: _____

Launched In: _____ First Flight: _____

✈ Weather ✈

Clean ☐   Sunny ☐   Stormy ☐   Rainy ☐   Cloudy ☐

✈ Equipment Used ✈

_____

_____

_____

✈ Notes ✈

_____

_____

_____

 Aircraft Spotted ✈

Date/Time: _____ Where/Location: _____

Airport Details: _____

✈ Aircraft Information ✈

Aircraft Name: _____ Engine Type: _____

Aircraft Model: _____ Engine No: _____

Aircraft Type: _____ Livery: _____

Aircraft Weight: _____ Height: _____

Aircraft Capacity: _____ Wing Shape: _____

Aircraft Length: _____ Fuseiage Diameter: _____

Wing Area: _____ Based On: _____

Launched In: _____ First Flight: _____

✈ Weather ✈

Clean ☐   Sunny ☐   Stormy ☐   Rainy ☐   Cloudy ☐

✈ Equipment Used ✈

_____

_____

_____

✈ Notes ✈

_____

_____

_____

✈ Aircraft Spotted ✈

Date/Time: _ _ _ _ _ _ _ _ _ _ _ _ _ Where/Location: _ _ _ _ _ _ _ _ _ _ _

Airport Details: _

✈ Aircraft Information ✈

Aircraft Name: _ _ _ _ _ _ _ _ _ _ _ Engine Type: _ _ _ _ _ _ _ _ _ _ _

Aircraft Model: _ _ _ _ _ _ _ _ _ _ Engine No: _ _ _ _ _ _ _ _ _ _ _ _ _

Aircraft Type: _ _ _ _ _ _ _ _ _ _ _ Livery: _ _ _ _ _ _ _ _ _ _ _ _ _ _ _

Aircraft Weight: _ _ _ _ _ _ _ _ _ _ Height: _ _ _ _ _ _ _ _ _ _ _ _ _ _ _

Aircraft Capacity: _ _ _ _ _ _ _ _ Wing Shape: _ _ _ _ _ _ _ _ _ _ _ _ _

Aircraft Length: _ _ _ _ _ _ _ _ _ Fuseiage Diameter: _ _ _ _ _ _ _ _ _

Wing Area: _ _ _ _ _ _ _ _ _ _ _ _ _ Based On: _ _ _ _ _ _ _ _ _ _ _ _ _ _

Launched In: _ _ _ _ _ _ _ _ _ _ _ First Flight: _ _ _ _ _ _ _ _ _ _ _ _ _

✈ Weather ✈

Clean ☐   Sunny ☐   Stormy ☐   Rainy ☐   Cloudy ☐

✈ Equipment Used ✈

_ _

_ _

_ _

✈ Notes ✈

_ _

_ _

_ _

 Aircraft Spotted

Date/Time: _ _ _ _ _ _ _ _ _ _ _ _ _ _ _ Where/Location: _ _ _ _ _ _ _ _ _ _ _ _ _

Airport Details: _

✈ Aircraft Information ✈

Aircraft Name: _ _ _ _ _ _ _ _ _ _ _ _ _ Engine Type: _ _ _ _ _ _ _ _ _ _ _ _ _ _

Aircraft Model: _ _ _ _ _ _ _ _ _ _ _ _ _ Engine No: _ _ _ _ _ _ _ _ _ _ _ _ _ _ _

Aircraft Type: _ _ _ _ _ _ _ _ _ _ _ _ _ _ Livery: _ _ _ _ _ _ _ _ _ _ _ _ _ _ _ _ _

Aircraft Weight: _ _ _ _ _ _ _ _ _ _ _ _ _ Height: _ _ _ _ _ _ _ _ _ _ _ _ _ _ _ _ _

Aircraft Capacity: _ _ _ _ _ _ _ _ _ _ _ _ Wing Shape: _ _ _ _ _ _ _ _ _ _ _ _ _ _

Aircraft Length: _ _ _ _ _ _ _ _ _ _ _ _ _ Fuseiage Diameter: _ _ _ _ _ _ _ _ _ _

Wing Area: _ _ _ _ _ _ _ _ _ _ _ _ _ _ _ _ Based On: _ _ _ _ _ _ _ _ _ _ _ _ _ _ _

Launched In: _ _ _ _ _ _ _ _ _ _ _ _ _ _ _ First Flight: _ _ _ _ _ _ _ _ _ _ _ _ _ _

✈ Weather ✈

Clean ☐   Sunny ☐   Stormy ☐   Rainy ☐   Cloudy ☐

✈ Equipment Used ✈

_ _

_ _

_ _

✈ Notes ✈

_ _

_ _

_ _

✈ Aircraft Spotted ✈

Date/Time: _ _ _ _ _ _ _ _ _ _ _ _ _ Where/Location: _ _ _ _ _ _ _ _ _ _ _

Airport Details: _

✈ Aircraft Information ✈

Aircraft Name: _ _ _ _ _ _ _ _ _ _ _ _ Engine Type: _ _ _ _ _ _ _ _ _ _ _

Aircraft Model: _ _ _ _ _ _ _ _ _ _ _ _ Engine No: _ _ _ _ _ _ _ _ _ _ _ _

Aircraft Type: _ _ _ _ _ _ _ _ _ _ _ _ _ Livery: _ _ _ _ _ _ _ _ _ _ _ _ _ _

Aircraft Weight: _ _ _ _ _ _ _ _ _ _ _ _ Height: _ _ _ _ _ _ _ _ _ _ _ _ _ _

Aircraft Capacity: _ _ _ _ _ _ _ _ _ _ _ Wing Shape: _ _ _ _ _ _ _ _ _ _ _

Aircraft Length: _ _ _ _ _ _ _ _ _ _ _ _ Fuseiage Diameter: _ _ _ _ _ _ _ _

Wing Area: _ _ _ _ _ _ _ _ _ _ _ _ _ _ _ Based On: _ _ _ _ _ _ _ _ _ _ _ _

Launched In: _ _ _ _ _ _ _ _ _ _ _ _ _ _ First Flight: _ _ _ _ _ _ _ _ _ _ _

✈ Weather ✈

Clean ☐   Sunny ☐   Stormy ☐   Rainy ☐   Cloudy ☐

✈ Equipment Used ✈

_ _

_ _

_ _

✈ Notes ✈

_ _

_ _

_ _

✈ Aircraft Spotted ✈

Date/Time: _____ Where/Location: _____

Airport Details: _____

✈ Aircraft Information ✈

Aircraft Name: _____ Engine Type: _____

Aircraft Model: _____ Engine No: _____

Aircraft Type: _____ Livery: _____

Aircraft Weight: _____ Height: _____

Aircraft Capacity: _____ Wing Shape: _____

Aircraft Length: _____ Fuseiage Diameter: _____

Wing Area: _____ Based On: _____

Launched In: _____ First Flight: _____

✈ Weather ✈

Clean ☐   Sunny ☐   Stormy ☐   Rainy ☐   Cloudy ☐

✈ Equipment Used ✈

_____

_____

_____

✈ Notes ✈

_____

_____

_____

✈ Aircraft Spotted ✈

Date/Time:_____ Where/Location:_____

Airport Details:_____

✈ Aircraft Information ✈

Aircraft Name:_____ Engine Type:_____

Aircraft Model:_____ Engine No:_____

Aircraft Type:_____ Livery:_____

Aircraft Weight:_____ Height:_____

Aircraft Capacity:_____ Wing Shape:_____

Aircraft Length:_____ Fuseiage Diameter:_____

Wing Area:_____ Based On:_____

Launched In:_____ First Flight:_____

✈ Weather ✈

Clean ☐   Sunny ☐   Stormy ☐   Rainy ☐   Cloudy ☐

✈ Equipment Used ✈

_____

_____

_____

✈ Notes ✈

_____

_____

_____

✈ Aircraft Spotted ✈

Date/Time: _____ Where/Location: _____

Airport Details: _____

✈ Aircraft Information ✈

Aircraft Name: _____ Engine Type: _____

Aircraft Model: _____ Engine No: _____

Aircraft Type: _____ Livery: _____

Aircraft Weight: _____ Height: _____

Aircraft Capacity: _____ Wing Shape: _____

Aircraft Length: _____ Fuseiage Diameter: _____

Wing Area: _____ Based On: _____

Launched In: _____ First Flight: _____

✈ Weather ✈

Clean ☐   Sunny ☐   Stormy ☐   Rainy ☐   Cloudy ☐

✈ Equipment Used ✈

_____

_____

_____

✈ Notes ✈

_____

_____

_____

✈ Aircraft Spotted ✈

Date/Time: _____ Where/Location: _____

Airport Details: _____

✈ Aircraft Information ✈

Aircraft Name: _____ Engine Type: _____

Aircraft Model: _____ Engine No: _____

Aircraft Type: _____ Livery: _____

Aircraft Weight: _____ Height: _____

Aircraft Capacity: _____ Wing Shape: _____

Aircraft Length: _____ Fuseiage Diameter: _____

Wing Area: _____ Based On: _____

Launched In: _____ First Flight: _____

✈ Weather ✈

Clean ☐   Sunny ☐   Stormy ☐   Rainy ☐   Cloudy ☐

✈ Equipment Used ✈

_____

_____

_____

✈ Notes ✈

_____

_____

_____

✈ Aircraft Spotted ✈

Date/Time: _____ Where/Location: _____

Airport Details: _____

✈ Aircraft Information ✈

Aircraft Name: _____ Engine Type: _____

Aircraft Model: _____ Engine No: _____

Aircraft Type: _____ Livery: _____

Aircraft Weight: _____ Height: _____

Aircraft Capacity: _____ Wing Shape: _____

Aircraft Length: _____ Fuseiage Diameter: _____

Wing Area: _____ Based On: _____

Launched In: _____ First Flight: _____

✈ Weather ✈

Clean ☐   Sunny ☐   Stormy ☐   Rainy ☐   Cloudy ☐

✈ Equipment Used ✈

_____

_____

_____

✈ Notes ✈

_____

_____

_____

✈ Aircraft Spotted ✈

Date/Time: _____ Where/Location: _____

Airport Details: _____

✈ Aircraft Information ✈

Aircraft Name: _____ Engine Type: _____

Aircraft Model: _____ Engine No: _____

Aircraft Type: _____ Livery: _____

Aircraft Weight: _____ Height: _____

Aircraft Capacity: _____ Wing Shape: _____

Aircraft Length: _____ Fuseiage Diameter: _____

Wing Area: _____ Based On: _____

Launched In: _____ First Flight: _____

✈ Weather ✈

Clean ☐   Sunny ☐   Stormy ☐   Rainy ☐   Cloudy ☐

✈ Equipment Used ✈

_____

_____

_____

✈ Notes ✈

_____

_____

_____

✈ Aircraft Spotted ✈

Date/Time: _____ Where/Location: _____

Airport Details: _____

✈ Aircraft Information ✈

Aircraft Name: _____ Engine Type: _____

Aircraft Model: _____ Engine No: _____

Aircraft Type: _____ Livery: _____

Aircraft Weight: _____ Height: _____

Aircraft Capacity: _____ Wing Shape: _____

Aircraft Length: _____ Fuseiage Diameter: _____

Wing Area: _____ Based On: _____

Launched In: _____ First Flight: _____

✈ Weather ✈

Clean ☐   Sunny ☐   Stormy ☐   Rainy ☐   Cloudy ☐

✈ Equipment Used ✈

_____

_____

_____

✈ Notes ✈

_____

_____

_____

✈ Aircraft Spotted ✈

Date/Time: _____ Where/Location: _____

Airport Details: _____

✈ Aircraft Information ✈

Aircraft Name: _____ Engine Type: _____

Aircraft Model: _____ Engine No: _____

Aircraft Type: _____ Livery: _____

Aircraft Weight: _____ Height: _____

Aircraft Capacity: _____ Wing Shape: _____

Aircraft Length: _____ Fuseiage Diameter: _____

Wing Area: _____ Based On: _____

Launched In: _____ First Flight: _____

✈ Weather ✈

Clean ☐   Sunny ☐   Stormy ☐   Rainy ☐   Cloudy ☐

✈ Equipment Used ✈

✈ Notes ✈

✈ Aircraft Spotted ✈

Date/Time: _____ Where/Location: _____

Airport Details: _____

✈ Aircraft Information ✈

Aircraft Name: _____ Engine Type: _____

Aircraft Model: _____ Engine No: _____

Aircraft Type: _____ Livery: _____

Aircraft Weight: _____ Height: _____

Aircraft Capacity: _____ Wing Shape: _____

Aircraft Length: _____ Fuseiage Diameter: _____

Wing Area: _____ Based On: _____

Launched In: _____ First Flight: _____

✈ Weather ✈

Clean ☐   Sunny ☐   Stormy ☐   Rainy ☐   Cloudy ☐

✈ Equipment Used ✈

_____

_____

_____

✈ Notes ✈

_____

_____

_____

✈ Aircraft Spotted ✈

Date/Time: _____ Where/Location: _____

Airport Details: _____

✈ Aircraft Information ✈

Aircraft Name: _____ Engine Type: _____

Aircraft Model: _____ Engine No: _____

Aircraft Type: _____ Livery: _____

Aircraft Weight: _____ Height: _____

Aircraft Capacity: _____ Wing Shape: _____

Aircraft Length: _____ Fuseiage Diameter: _____

Wing Area: _____ Based On: _____

Launched In: _____ First Flight: _____

✈ Weather ✈

Clean ☐   Sunny ☐   Stormy ☐   Rainy ☐   Cloudy ☐

✈ Equipment Used ✈

_____

_____

_____

✈ Notes ✈

_____

_____

_____

✈ Aircraft Spotted ✈

Date/Time: _____ Where/Location: _____

Airport Details: _____

✈ Aircraft Information ✈

Aircraft Name: _____ Engine Type: _____

Aircraft Model: _____ Engine No: _____

Aircraft Type: _____ Livery: _____

Aircraft Weight: _____ Height: _____

Aircraft Capacity: _____ Wing Shape: _____

Aircraft Length: _____ Fuseiage Diameter: _____

Wing Area: _____ Based On: _____

Launched In: _____ First Flight: _____

✈ Weather ✈

Clean ☐   Sunny ☐   Stormy ☐   Rainy ☐   Cloudy ☐

✈ Equipment Used ✈

_____

_____

_____

✈ Notes ✈

_____

_____

_____

✈ Aircraft Spotted ✈

Date/Time: _____ Where/Location: _____

Airport Details: _____

✈ Aircraft Information ✈

Aircraft Name: _____ Engine Type: _____

Aircraft Model: _____ Engine No: _____

Aircraft Type: _____ Livery: _____

Aircraft Weight: _____ Height: _____

Aircraft Capacity: _____ Wing Shape: _____

Aircraft Length: _____ Fuseiage Diameter: _____

Wing Area: _____ Based On: _____

Launched In: _____ First Flight: _____

✈ Weather ✈

Clean ☐   Sunny ☐   Stormy ☐   Rainy ☐   Cloudy ☐

✈ Equipment Used ✈

✈ Notes ✈

Printed in Great Britain
by Amazon

83743046R00058